Shimmy with my Granny

Family Poems

Chosen and Illustrated by
Sarah Garland

MACDONALD YOUNG BOOKS

The Hot-Air Monster

I hate the Hot-Air Monster,
I hate its boiling breath,
I hate the way it finds me,
I fight it to the death.

It comes out after bath-time,
it can't run very fast,
so I hide behind the sofa
to escape its fiery blast.

Mum finds me there and grabs me,
I twist between her knees,
she holds the Hot-Air Monster
and points its nose at me.

I yank up my pyjamas
to cover all my hair,
it noses down my armhole
and blows its fire in there.

Red hot scalding fury
burns my ears and head
but I battle with the monster
until it's time for bed.

I hate the Hot-Air Monster,
I hate its boiling breath,
I hate the way it finds me,
I fight it to the death.

Ellen Phethean

First published in Great Britain in 1999 by
Macdonald Young Books
an imprint of Wayland Publishers Ltd
61 Western Road
Hove
East Sussex
BN3 1JD

Find Macdonald Young Books on the internet at http://www.myb.co.uk

Printed and bound in Belgium by Proost
British Library Cataloguing in Publication Data available

ISBN: 0 7500 2764 9

eggs
and bacon
sausages
fried bread
mushrooms
tomatoes
baked beans

Fry-Up!

When Mum says
'We're going to have a Fry-Up!'
Golly! How
my spirits fly up,
no mistake,
I feel like a Wedding
in the Land of Cake!

When Mum says
'I feel like doing a Fry-Up!'
I feel great
as any High-Up,
no mistake,
I feel like an Ice-Cream
with a Chocolate Flake!

When Mum says,
'It's time to have a Fry-Up!'
all my tears
quite quickly dry up,
no mistake,
**nothing beats a Fry-Up
no, nothing you could ever
broil or boil or bake!**

Gavin Ewart

Leaky Baby

Our brand new baby's sprung a leak!
He's dripping like a spout.
We'd better send him back
Before the guarantee runs out.

Kaye Umansky

Getting Rid of My Sister

I put my little sister out with the rubbish
and waited for the bin men to come.
But instead of taking her to the rubbish tip
they gave her back to my mum.

Lindsay MacRae

from *Dahn the Plug'ole*

Your biby 'as fell dahn the plug'ole,
Your biby 'as gorn dahn the plug;
The poor little thing was so skinny and thin
'E oughter been barfed in a jug.

Anon.

from *The Eddystone Light*

Me father was the keeper of the Eddystone Light,
He married a mer-my-aid one night;
Out of the match came children three –
Two was fish and the other was me.   *Anon.*

Mr Kartoffel

Mr Kartoffel's a whimsical man;
He drinks his beer from a watering can,
And for no good reason that I can see
He fills his pockets with China tea.
He parts his hair with a knife and fork
And takes his ducks for a Sunday walk.

Says he, 'If my wife and I should choose
To wear our stockings outside our shoes,
Plant tulip bulbs in the baby's pram
And eat tobacco instead of jam,
And fill the bath with cauliflowers,
That's nobody's business at all but ours.'

James Reeves

Nan

My Nan is sitting
in her chair.
Butterflies are
in her hair.
In her lap
are golden eggs.
Purple stockings
on her legs.

On every finger
there's a ring.
Beside her ear
two angels sing.
Beneath her feet
a magic mat.
Above her head
an acrobat.

Against her knee
a tiger smiles.
My Nan's eyes
can see for miles.
She sits so tall,
so grand and pale,
I think she's in
a fairy tale.

Sarah Garland

Danny

Danny can
jump off the top of the small green cupboard
and on to the bed.
He's off his head.

Danny can
climb the old pine-tree in the yard
without looking down.
He's a clown.

Danny can
take a blue woolly blanket
and make a den.
He's nearly ten.

Danny can
beat my Uncle Mike at games
like draughts and chess.
His hair's a mess.

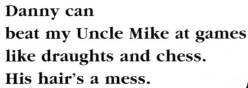

I can't jump or climb or build or win at games
But Danny's my favourite cousin
and he can.

Adèle Geras

I Want Mum

My Granny is all right.
In fact she's very nice.
But if I say it once
I think I'll say it twice
(especially at night)
I WANT MUM!

She rings me every day
(Mum does, I mean)
to hear the things I've done,
but Grandpa (who is fun)
says, 'Hey, all day you've been so cheerful
but on the phone you're tearful!'

Before we all get up
we have our tea in bed
and he pours me a cup
then watches anxiously
in case it's N S E
(Not Sweet Enough, you see)
or worse, T H (Too Hot)
and if I say it's not,
that it's J R (Just Right)
he then pretends to shout
'J R!' to all the houses,
East, West, North and South
his hands around his mouth
like a megaphone.

But on the telephone
all this fun we've had
comes out sounding sad.
The reason you can guess
(I said I'd say it twice)
I WANT MUM!

It's when I wake at night
the bedclothes all a-jumble
'She's not here' I find
and I begin a mumble
which rises to a shout
and Granny runs to see me
(I told you she was kind)
and reads till I am dreamy.
It's good to hear her read
but it isn't her I need.
It's like a pain in the tum –
I WANT MUM!

P. J. Kavanagh

Pink!

On grey days
Rainy days
Boring can't go out days
I creep into my mummy's room
And count her sarees one by one

And think

When I grow up I'll wear

The yellow one for shopping
The orange one for cooking
The peach one for lounging about
The purple one for listening to music
The green one for going out to tea
The blue one for praying in the temple
The red one with gold for when I marry.

But for a day
A special day
The once a year birthday day
I'll dress up in my favourite one
My brightest one
Excitingest one
The one that is
Blinding
Pink
Pinker than
Pink
Truly awfully SHOCKING pink

And jump over the moon.

Jamila Gavin

D is for Dad. Dad's gone away.

I must be me. I go to stay with my Dad at weekends. It was odd to begin with but now it's OK.

Very sad? Sometimes. Don't know.

O is for Over. That starts with O. When they told me the news I was angry, and cried, and I shouted, "Don't go!"

R is for Rows. Mum yelling at Dad.

C for Commotion. Dad getting mad.

But now they're apart
they talk to each other
and that can't be bad.

E is for Ending. Is it the end?

Mum's still my mother. Dad's Dad. My friend.
Mum's playing football,
Dad's cooking tea,
it's really OK
being someone like me...

Vivian French

Dad

Dad is the dancingman,
The laughing-bear, the prickle-chin,
The tickle-fingers, jungle-roars,
Bucking bronco, rocking-horse,
The helicopter roundabout,
The beat-the-wind at swing-and-shout,
Goal-post, scary-ghost,
Climbing-Jack, humpty-back.

But sometimes he's
A go-away-please!
A snorey-snarl, a sprawly lump,

And I'm a kite without a string
Waiting for Dad to dance again.

Berlie Doherty

A Tough Question

'Why do all parents
Tell children the same old lie –
"You're loved equally" –
When it's clear they have favourites?'
Yukio asked his grandad.

'Ah,' said the old man
(He was fond of saying 'Ah'),
'It's not quite a lie,
It's half the truth. The most loved
Is often not the best loved.

Do you follow my meaning?'
'No,' said Yukio, 'I don't.'
'But you will one day.'
'Grandad, I think you're crazy.'
'Ah, that's why you're my favourite!'

James Michie

My Little Brother

When I'm in the playground
with my little brother,
my Aunt Lucy chats to my mother.
I want to play, but that doesn't matter
they say, 'Keep an eye on Billy,
while we have a natter.'

Billy's off to the swings,
he's always in a rush,
I lift him on the swing,
and then I have to push.
I push and I push,
but he wants to go higher,
I push so hard
my arms start to tire.

'I can't push any more!' I shout to my mother,
'I'm really getting fed up with my little brother!
He won't get off the swings!
I don't know what to do!'
But she says, 'Let him have another go,
he's littler than you!'

So I say my arms are tired,
and he'll have to decide
what he wants to do next,
and he points to the slide.

I guide him up the ladder
to make sure he doesn't fall,
then I run to the shute,
and I wait for him to call
'I'm coming!' – then I have to catch him
before he hits the ground,
then he's off again, and on the steps
a second time around

and a third and a fourth, till I shout to my mother,
'I'm really getting fed up with my little brother!
He won't get off the slide, I don't know what to do!'
She says, 'Let him have another go, he's littler than you!'

So I say my legs are tired,
and Billy starts to moan –
he wants a game of football –
he can play it on his own!
But when Billy kicks the ball
and it bounces on the ground
two bigger boys just grab it
and they're kicking it around.

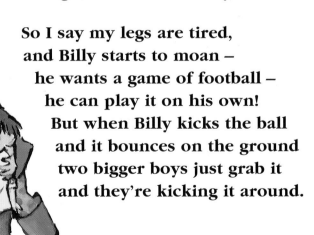

They won't let Billy play with it, but I know what to do –
I shout, 'Let my brother have a go, he's littler than you!'

Pat Hutchins

Hamster

My hamster's very funny
But I do wish he could talk
And tell me why he briskly
Takes his biscuit for a walk.

My hamster cleans his front end
With his fore-paws every day,
He grooms his ears and whiskers
In a serious sort of way.
But his back end, I'm afraid,
Is like a bit of raggy mat,
And when he runs around it goes
Widdle-waddle-pat.

On the day my hamster died
I sat and watched the rain outside
Pour and pour and pour.

I didn't know what things were for
And so
I sat and cried.

Joyce Dunbar

High Heels

I wonder
how it feels
to wear high heels
like my big sister?

Coz I'm smaller
I have to wait
longer
for high heels
to make me taller.

I wonder
how it feels
to wear high heels
and have corns
on your toes
and a blister?

I suppose
I'd better
ask my big sister.

John Agard

Lucky Lennie

Lucky Lennie is my name,
I'm gazing at the ceiling.
My dad is hiding somewhere
while I have a dental filling.

(Dad's voice:)
'You're so lucky, Lennie,
you just don't know your luck.
When I was your age, Lennie,
you had to have some pluck
to press the dentist's doorbell,
and climb the dentist's stair,
to pretend to read a comic,
then to get into his chair.
They used a sort of road drill then,
and sometimes it got stuck.

You're so lucky, Lennie,
you just don't know your luck.
He'd hoover up your tongue
and shovel up the bits,
and lever with a pickaxe
with a bucket for the spits,
then when he'd made a whopping hole
he'd cram it with some muck.
You're so lucky, Lennie,
you just don't know your luck.'

(I say:)
'Come out now, Dad, it's over.
It really wasn't bad.
And I didn't feel a thing,
not a thing, Dad.

Sarah Garland

They Chose Me

I have two mothers,
My birth mother and my Mum.
I have two fathers,
My blood father and my Dad.

But of all the babies born
In the whole wide world
My Mum and Dad chose me.

I have two days,
My Birthday and my Chosen Day.
I get two cakes
And have my friends to tea.

But of all the babies born
In the whole wide world,
My Mum and Dad chose me.

I am the one,
The child they went to find,
I am the one
To make their family,

For of all the babies born
In the whole wide world,
My Mum and Dad chose me.

Jamila Gavin

Baby's Drinking Song

Sip a little
Sup a little
From your little
Cup a little
Sup a little
Sip a little
Put it to your
Lip a little
Tip a little
Tap a little
Not into your
Lap or it'll
Drip a little
Drop a little
On the table
Top a little.

James Kirkup

*To be spoken three times,
each time faster than the last.*

from *Hugger Mugger*

I'd sooner be
Jumped and thumped and dumped,

I'd sooner be
Slugged and mugged. . . than *hugged*. . .

And clobbered with a slobbering
Kiss by my Auntie Jean:

You know what I mean:

Whenever she comes to stay,
You know you're bound
To get one.
> A quick
> short
> peck
> would
> be
> OK
But this is a
> Whacking great
> Smacking great
> *Wet* one!

Kit Wright

Who's a Lovely Girl?

Well, who's a lovely girl then?
(Not me, you stupid bat.)
And who's got shiny hair then?
(You'd think I was the cat.)

You're so much like your mummy.
(I think I'm just like me.)
With little bits of grandma.
(I have to disagree.)

And, wow, you have grown taller!
(That's what we humans do.)
And who's a clever girl then?
(Obviously not you.)

Steve Turner

The Speak Mum Speaks

the speak Mum speaks
when she's on the phone
I asked her one time
where it comes from
she says it's the speak
of her friends from home

the speak Mum speaks
like floating and laughing
and the words are bubbling
whispering hurrying
she says it's the speak
of where she comes from

the speak Mum speaks
like singing and dancing
like friends holding hands
going out to playtime
like a playground
with everyone jumping

I sit small and say nothing
I listen and listen
to the speak Mum speaks
flashing and shining
like jewel diamonds
and I want some

Helen Dunmore

Bedtime

When I go upstairs to bed,
I usually give a loud cough.
This is to scare The Monster off.

When I come to my room,
I usually slam the door right back.
This is to squash The Man in Black
Who sometimes hides there.

Nor do I walk to the bed,
But usually run and jump instead.
This is to stop The Hand –
Which is under there all right –
From grabbing my ankles.

Allan Ahlberg

Exactly Like a 'V'

When my brother Tommy
Sleeps in bed with me
He doubles up
And makes
himself
exactly
like
a
V

And 'cause the bed is not so wide
A part of him is on my side.

Abram Bunn Ross

Dreams

Here we are all, by day;
by night we are hurled
By dreams, each one,
into a several world.

Robert Herrick

Nursery Rhyme

Hush-a-bye, baby,
your milk's in the tin,
Mummy has got you
a nice sitter-in;

Hush-a-bye, baby,
now don't get a frown
while Mummy and Daddy
are out on the town.

Anon.

Lullaby

Sleep little baby, clean as a nut,
Your fingers uncurl and your eyes
  are shut.
Your life was ours, which is with you.
Go on your journey. We go too.

The bat is flying round the house
Like an umbrella turned into a mouse.
The moon is astonished and so are
  the sheep:
Their bells have come to send you to sleep.

Oh be our rest, our hopeful start.
Turn your head to my beating heart.
Sleep little baby, clean as a nut,
Your fingers uncurl and your eyes are shut.

Elizabeth Jennings

Award-winning author, Sarah Garland, has written and illustrated over forty picture books and adventure stories for children. Sarah is best known for her warm and witty portrayals of family relationships. It is not surprising that, as compiler and illustrator of her first collection of poetry, she has chosen poems that reflect the ups and downs of family life.

Sarah Garland and Macdonald Young Books would like to thank all the poets who have given permission for copyright material to be included in this collection:

'A Poem Just Like This' © Kit Wright, 1984

'A Tough Question' © James Michie, 1999

'Baby's Drinking Song' © James Kirkup, 1998

'Bedtime' (p93, 12 lines) from *Please Mrs Butler* by Allan Ahlberg (Kestrel Books, 1983) © Allan Ahlberg 1983

'D is for Dad' © Vivian French, 1998

'Dad' © Berlie Doherty, from *Walking on Air* (Harper Collins, 1993)

'Danny' © Adèle Geras, 1999

'Fry-up' © Margo Ewart, 1992

'Getting Rid of My Sister' (p21, 4 lines) from *You Canny Shove Your Granny off a Bus* by Lindsay Macrae (Viking, 1995) © Lindsay Macrae, 1995

'Hamster' © Joyce Dunbar, 1999

'High Heels' By kind permission of John Agard c/o Caroline Sheldon Literacy Agency: 'High Heels' from *I Din Do Nuttin* (Bodley Head, 1983)

'Hot-air Monster' © Ellen Phethean, 1998

'Hugger Mugger' (pp91–93, 45 lines) from *Hot Dog and Other Poems* by Kit Wright (Kestrel, 1981) © Kit Wright

'I Want Mum' © P.J. Kavanagh, 1998

'Leaky Baby' © Kaye Umansky, 1999

'Lucky Lennie' © Sarah Garland, 1999

'Lullaby' © Elizabeth Jennings from *Poets in Hand – a Puffin Quintet of Poets* (Puffin, 1985)

'Mr Kartoffel' © James Reeves from *Complete Poems for Children* (Heinemann). Reprinted by permission of the James Reeves Estate.

'My Little Brother' © Pat Hutchins, 1998

'Nan' © Sarah Garland, 1999

'Pink!' © Jamila Gavin, 1999

'The Speak Mum Speaks' © Helen Dunmore, 1999

'They Chose Me' © Jamila Gavin, 1999

'Who's a Lovely Girl?' from *The Day I Fell Down the Toilet*, © Steve Turner, 1996 (Lion Publishing plc) Reprinted by permission.

Every effort has been made to trace and contact copyright holders. The publishers will be pleased to make any necessary corrections in future reprints, in the event of an error or omission in the use of copyright material.

Translation from the Shona language for *The Speak Mum Speaks*: 'How are things there?... I'm fine... Look after yourself!'